Working with Nonprofit Organizations

Margaret Henderson, Lydian Altman,
Suzanne Julian, Gordan P. Whitaker,
and Eileen R. Youens

UNC
SCHOOL OF
GOVERNMENT

About the Series

Local Government Board Builders offers local elected leaders practical advice on how to effectively lead and govern. Each of the booklets in this series provides a topic overview, specific tips on effective practice, and worksheets and reflection questions to help local elected leaders improve their work. The series focuses on common activities for local governing boards, such as selecting and appointing committees and advisory boards, planning for the future, making better decisions, improving board accountability, and effectively engaging stakeholders in public decisions.

Vaughn Mamlin Upshaw, lecturer in public administration and government at the UNC School of Government, is the series editor.

Other Books in the Series

Leading Your Governing Board: A Guide for Mayors and County Board Chairs, Vaughn Mamlin Upshaw, 2009

A Model Code of Ethics for North Carolina Local Elected Officials, A. Fleming Bell, II, 2010

Creating and Maintaining Effective Local Government Citizen Advisory Committees, Vaughn Mamlin Upshaw, 2010

Public Outreach and Participation, John B. Stephens, Ricardo S. Morse, and Kelley T. O'Brien, forthcoming in 2010

The School of Government at the University of North Carolina at Chapel Hill works to improve the lives of North Carolinians by engaging in practical scholarship that helps public officials and citizens understand and improve state and local government. Established in 1931 as the Institute of Government, the School provides educational, advisory, and research services for state and local governments. The School of Government is also home to a nationally ranked graduate program in public administration and specialized centers focused on information technology, environmental finance, and civic education for youth.

As the largest university-based local government training, advisory, and research organization in the United States, the School of Government offers up to 200 courses, seminars, and specialized conferences for more than 12,000 public officials each year. In addition, faculty members annually publish approximately fifty books, book chapters, bulletins, and other reference works related to state and local government. Each day that the General Assembly is in session, the School produces the *Daily Bulletin*, which reports on the day's activities for members of the legislature and others who need to follow the course of legislation.

The Master of Public Administration Program is a full-time, two-year program that serves up to sixty students annually. It consistently ranks among the best public administration graduate programs in the country, particularly in city management. With courses ranging from public policy analysis to ethics and management, the program educates leaders for local, state, and federal governments and nonprofit organizations.

Operating support for the School of Government's programs and activities comes from many sources, including state appropriations, local government membership dues, private contributions, publication sales, course fees, and service contracts. Visit www.sog.unc.edu or call 919.966.5381 for more information on the School's courses, publications, programs, and services.

Michael R. Smith, DEAN
Thomas H. Thornburg, SENIOR ASSOCIATE DEAN
Frayda S. Bluestein, ASSOCIATE DEAN FOR FACULTY DEVELOPMENT
Todd A. Nicolet, ASSOCIATE DEAN FOR OPERATIONS
Ann Cary Simpson, ASSOCIATE DEAN FOR DEVELOPMENT AND COMMUNICATIONS
Bradley G. Volk, ASSOCIATE DEAN FOR ADMINISTRATION

FACULTY

Gregory S. Allison	Alyson A. Grine	Christopher B. McLaughlin	Carl W. Stenberg III
David N. Ammons	Norma Houston (on leave)	Kara A. Millonzi	John B. Stephens
Ann M. Anderson	Cheryl Daniels Howell	Jill D. Moore	Charles A. Szypszak
A. Fleming Bell, II	Jeffrey A. Hughes	Jonathan Q. Morgan	Shannon H. Tufts
Maureen M. Berner	Willow S. Jacobson	Ricardo S. Morse	Vaughn Mamlin Upshaw
Mark F. Botts	Robert P. Joyce	C. Tyler Mulligan	A. John Vogt
Joan G. Brannon	Kenneth L. Joyner	David W. Owens	Aimee N. Wall
Michael Crowell	Diane M. Juffras	William C. Rivenbark	Jeffrey B. Welty
Shea Riggsbee Denning	David M. Lawrence	Dale J. Roenigk	Richard B. Whisnant
James C. Drennan	Dona G. Lewandowski	John Rubin	Gordon P. Whitaker
Richard D. Ducker	James M. Markham	John L. Saxon	Eileen R. Youens
Robert L. Farb	Janet Mason	Jessica Smith	
Joseph S. Ferrell	Laurie L. Mesibov	Karl W. Smith	

Printed in the United States of America
14 13 12 11 10   1 2 3 4 5
ISBN 978-1-56011-658-5
♾ This publication is printed on permanent, acid-free paper in compliance with the North Carolina General Statutes.
♺ Printed on recycled paper

Contents

Introduction

Over the past three decades, local governments all across the United States have increased their involvement with nonprofit organizations.[1] Many governments face the challenges of providing more and better services while being constrained by difficult fiscal limits. To help meet these challenges, many have involved nonprofits in service delivery, drawing on these organizations' volunteers and private financial resources as well as their greater flexibility of action. Some nonprofits have also become skilled advocates for the clients they serve, making persuasive appeals for public funding of their work or otherwise helping shape governments' priorities.

Local governments can work effectively with nonprofits to address public needs by funding nonprofits, providing them property, sharing training opportunities, providing expertise or other types of in-kind assistance, or partnering with them to jointly develop and implement public service programs. Government funding of nonprofits—through direct appropriations, grants, or purchase-of-service contracts—is the most common sort of continuing relationship between the two types of organizations. This guidebook will focus primarily on the basic questions North Carolina's local governments should ask themselves when deciding whether and how to fund nonprofits. If the governing board is considering an ongoing partnership with a nonprofit, many of these same considerations will apply.

1. This guidebook has been written for elected officials of municipal and county governments, but governing officials of other kinds of public entities, such as councils of government, might find the information useful as well.

A *nonprofit* is an organization that uses its surplus funds to support its stated purpose rather than distributing those funds to owners or shareholders. Nonprofits vary significantly in size, purpose, and sophistication. Although commonly referred to as "charities," nonprofits can be anything from a volunteer fire department to a private university to a church. In this guidebook, a "nonprofit" refers to a community-based organization that provides some kind of public service that supports particular local government interests. These types of nonprofits usually fall under Internal Revenue Code § 501(c)(3).

Why Fund Nonprofits?

North Carolina law provides that public funds be spent only for public purposes.[1] Thus, local governing boards need to understand that funds provided to a nonprofit organization (like any government expenditure) are to be used for purposes for which the local government has authority to spend funds. A local government may choose to fund nonprofits to provide for many such "public purposes."

One possible reason for funding nonprofits is to support the work nonprofits do to better the community. For example, a city may want to aid assistance to homeless people by helping fund a homeless shelter or a community kitchen operated by a nonprofit. A county may want to encourage new employment opportunities by helping fund an economic development corporation or a chamber of commerce.

Second, a local government might fund a nonprofit so that the nonprofit can provide specific programs or services. Instead of building and staffing a swimming pool, a town might decide to partner with a nonprofit organization and help fund its capital or operating expenditures for the pool. Instead of operating an animal shelter, a county might contract with a nonprofit to do so. Rather than funding a broad range of valuable community services, elected officials may decide to tie their expenditures to programs that directly support a specific goal of the jurisdiction's strategic plan. For example, if economic development is a primary goal of a particular county, that county's funding for nonprofits might focus on economic development, literacy, and subsidized child care to enable parents to take jobs. If the county's priority is youth development, it might support nonprofits that provide after-school programs, tutoring, or recreation opportunities.

Finally, local governments might fund nonprofits to increase the impact of public expenditures. Even small nonprofits can multiply the effects of public spending by leveraging

---

1. N.C. CONST. ART. V, § 2(1), (7); Hughey v. Cloninger, 37 N.C. App. 107, 245 S.E.2d 543 (1978), *aff'd*, 297 N.C. 86, 253 S.E.2d 898 (1979). The North Carolina General Statutes also specifically authorize local governments to "contract with and appropriate money to any person, association, or corporation, in order to carry out any public purpose that the [local government] is authorized by law to engage in." N.C. GEN. STAT. (hereinafter G.S.) § 153A-449 (counties), G.S. 160A-20.1 (cities).

other resources. For example, by using volunteers in an efficient and effective manner, a nonprofit can increase the impact of each local government dollar. Many nonprofits also receive donations, grants, sales receipts, or other funds, thus expanding the work supported by local government funding.

Tips for Deciding Whether to Fund Nonprofits

Nonprofits may deliver services more effectively or at less cost than governments. When deciding whether to provide funds to a nonprofit, the local government should ask itself the following:

- Can the nonprofit supplement public funds with contributions of time, expertise, and money from volunteers and other donors?
- Can the nonprofit move more flexibly or quickly than the government to address a community need?
- Is the nonprofit in a position to build a sense of partnership or encourage civic participation by involving volunteers, neighbors, or others known and trusted by a particular community?
- Can the nonprofit provide specialized expertise in community issues or a specific population because of its mission and experience?
- How can the nonprofit augment, complement, or fill gaps in government services?
- What is our local government's experience working with nonprofit organizations?
- What has worked well? What could be improved?
- How is the nonprofit perceived within the community?

Ways to Fund Nonprofits

The variety of options local governments have to fund nonprofits is described below.

Purchase of Services

Local governments may purchase services from nonprofit organizations in the same way they do from other entities. These purchases can be made through the unit's regular processes and may have the same terms and conditions as those regularly imposed on the unit's other service providers. The North Carolina General Statutes do not require bidding for the purchase of services. In fact, the process used to acquire these services is left to the local government.[1]

Grants

A grant is a provision of funds in exchange for a promise by the grantee to perform certain prescribed activities or to produce particular results. The process for awarding grants is usually different from the process for purchasing services. Competition is typically structured differently, and in many cases a grant may describe the required services in less detail than a contract for the purchase of services.

Another important difference between grants and the purchase of services is that local government grants often involve "pass-through" funds from the state or federal government. Funds and eligibility standards for these grants originate with the state or federal government but the funds are awarded to nonprofits by local government. These types

---

1. For four specific types of services—architectural, engineering, surveying, and construction-management-at-risk—North Carolina local governments must use a qualifications-based selection process to choose a service provider. G.S. 143-64.31. Even then, local governments may exempt themselves from this process if they do so in writing (and provide a justification if the fee for the service is $30,000 or more). G.S. 143-64.32.

of grants may require that the local government comply with reporting, accounting, and other requirements from the granting entity and that the local government use specified procedures for awarding the grants. With other kinds of contracts, the local government has more discretion to include terms and requirements as it deems appropriate.

Appropriations

Like a grant or service purchase, a direct appropriation may be made to a nonprofit organization to carry out any activity for which the local government is authorized to spend money. An appropriation is a budgetary action in which the governing board approves the expenditure of funds for a particular purpose. Although an appropriation may not be accompanied by the same paperwork as grants and purchases, it really should be treated in the same way. In practice, an appropriation is likely to be less specific than a grant or other contract and may simply take the form of a lump-sum payment by the local government to the nonprofit. However, the local government and the nonprofit must ensure that the funds are used only for purposes the local government has authority to support. Many local governments enter into contracts with nonprofits that specify terms for using these government-appropriated funds.

Other Kinds of Support

Local governments also provide in-kind support to nonprofits by contributing property or personnel assistance to programs provided by those nonprofits. For example, a local government might include nonprofit staff in its training programs or use its purchasing power to purchase goods or services on behalf of the nonprofit for use in programs the local government has authority to fund.[2] Further, a local government may make the expertise of its staff available to the nonprofit as a form of in-kind assistance that might save money for both the local government and the nonprofit. In each case the basic legal limitations on these types of in-kind assistance are the same as those discussed above. If the activity of the nonprofit is one the local government has legal authority to support, that government can provide in-kind assistance in a wide variety of ways.

---

2. G.S. 160A-279 and G.S. 160A-280 give cities and counties the authority to donate property to nonprofits carrying out a public purpose.

Legal Issues in Funding Nonprofits

Although local governments and nonprofits work together or interact in many circumstances without contracting, contracts are the most common vehicles for these collaborations. The questions and answers in this section explain the basic principles behind the legal limitations on government contracts with (and other support for) nonprofits.

1. What authority do local governments have to contract with nonprofit organizations and what are the limitations on the exercise of that authority?

For North Carolina local governments, the authority to contract is directly related to the basic authority to spend money. A local government may contract for any purpose for which it may spend money. The three key legal limitations on the expenditure of funds by a local government are that (1) the expenditure be for a public purpose, (2) the activity supported be one in which the local government has statutory authority to engage, and (3) the expenditure must not be inconsistent with the laws or the constitution of the state or federal government. The next three questions discuss these limitations.

2. What is a public purpose?

The definition of *public purpose* is difficult to pin down. The North Carolina courts have used two guiding principles to determine whether a particular activity is for a public purpose: (1) whether the activity involves "a reasonable connection with the convenience and necessity of the [local government]" and (2) whether the activity "benefits the public generally, as opposed to special interests or persons." The courts have also offered at least two refinements of the second principle. First, it is not necessary to show that every citizen will benefit from an activity for it to be considered a public purpose. Furthermore, the fact that one or more private individuals benefit does not eliminate the public purpose. In other words, a private individual or business may directly benefit from a contract or an appropriation. This does not extinguish the public purpose as long as the public will benefit and the private benefit does not outweigh the public benefit.

3. Explain the requirement for "statutory authority." Must a statute specifically authorize the contract?

North Carolina local governments do not have inherent authority. They operate under authority delegated to them by the state legislature through enabling laws. So, in addition to serving a public purpose, a particular action of a local government (including an expenditure or a contract) must be authorized by a state statute.

This does not necessarily mean there must be a statute that specifically authorizes the local government to enter into a contract for every activity it might wish to support. The state constitution contains a general authorization for contracts with private entities. Thus, as long as a statute authorizes a particular activity, the local government may carry out the activity itself or contract with a third party to carry out all or part of the activity.

4. Are local governments prohibited from contracting with religious (faith-based) organizations?

No. Local governments may contract with faith-based nonprofits for services as long as those contracts do not violate the federal or state constitutions or other laws. Generally speaking, a contract with a faith-based group will be deemed lawful if the contract has a neutral purpose and effect both toward and among religions and avoids excessive government entanglement with religion. In other words, the terms of the contract must have the effect of safeguarding (1) the religious freedom of beneficiaries, both those who are willing to receive services from religious organizations and those who object to receiving services from such organizations and (2) the religious integrity and character of faith-based organizations willing to accept government funds to provide services to the needy.

5. **What, if any, limitations must a contract involving public funds impose on the activities of the religious organization? What limitations may the contract impose?**

Notwithstanding widespread thought to the contrary, there are few legal limitations on religious organizations that receive public funding for programs. Although the public funder may impose religion-neutral restrictions, the only generally applicable restriction is that public funds not be used to pay for worship services, sectarian instruction, or proselytization.

A common misperception is that the use of public funds in program delivery automatically subjects the faith-based institution to the same standards as the public funder. That is not so. Religious institutions retain their autonomy even when under contract with local governments. So, for example, religious organizations retain their right to use religious criteria in hiring, firing, and disciplining employees. Although it would be illegal for local government employers to discriminate in employment on the basis of religion, they may fund a religious group that does so.

6. **Do the rules about contracting apply regardless of whether government funding is a purchase of service, a grant, or an appropriation?**

Yes. Both the basic authority for local governments and the limitations discussed so far are the same regardless of the form of assistance being provided. Service purchase contracts, grants, appropriations, and in-kind contributions (such as donations of property or land) are all subject to the same limitations.

7. **Must a local government determine whether it can provide the service in-house before contracting with a private entity to provide the service?**

No, although some may do so as a matter of local discretion. There is no legal requirement or preference for performing functions or delivering services using public employees rather than through contracts with private entities. When bidding requirements apply, the local government must obtain competition from outside the local government.[1] In addition, some units of government have privatization or managed-competition programs in place, in which the units systematically compare the cost and the desirability of using

1. Bidding is required by statute for purchases of apparatus, materials, supplies, and equipment costing $30,000 or more and for construction and repair contracts costing $30,000 or more. G.S. 143-129, G.S. 143-131. In addition, North Carolina law requires local governments to solicit competition (using a qualifications-based selection process) for architectural, engineering, surveying, and construction-management-at-risk services, although local governments may exempt themselves from this process. G.S. 143-64.31, G.S. 143-64.32. Local government policies or practices may require bidding for other types of contracts as well.

the private sector for service delivery with the cost and the desirability of public delivery. These programs are implemented as a matter of local policy, however, and are not mandated by law.

8. What about conflicts of interest? For example, if a county commissioner also serves on the board of a nonprofit, is the county legally barred from contracting with that nonprofit?

State law makes it unlawful for a public official to benefit from a contract with the unit he or she represents.[2] For example, a local government generally may not contract with a business owned by one of its board members. A number of exceptions apply, however, including one that allows a limited amount of contracting in small jurisdictions. The conflict-of-interest laws do not apply if the public official does not receive any financial benefit from the contract. Also, a public official is not considered to have an interest in a contract if the official is an employee, rather than an owner, of the entity that contracts with the local government. So it is legal for a local government to contract with or provide other support to a nonprofit when a member of the local government's board is a volunteer (unpaid) member or salaried employee of the nonprofit board.

The board members and the employees of both the local government and the nonprofit always must consider the nonlegal issues that might arise when a person is involved on both sides of a contract. Negative publicity may stem from this type of transaction, and citizens as well as members of the nonprofit may question whether the board member or other person can adequately execute his or her responsibilities to both organizations, especially if a conflict was to arise over the contract. Thus even when the law does not prohibit a contract, avoiding it may be advisable if an ethical issue or a perception of conflict of interest might result.

9. May a local government donate property to a nonprofit or provide other in-kind support to nonprofit activities?

Yes. Subject to the requirements of public purpose and statutory authority, discussed in questions 1–3, local governments may provide in-kind support of whatever nature they choose. This includes not only the sale or the donation of property but also technical support or other assistance that may be provided using the unit's employees, building space, land, or equipment.

2. G.S. 14-234(a)(1).

Deciding to Fund Nonprofits

When local governments are deciding whether and how to fund nonprofits, approaching the issue deliberately can make the process smoother and more effective. Government officials want guidance when making tough funding decisions, especially when those decisions involve controversial, time-consuming, or passionate appeals from community-based nonprofit organizations. What community services do government officials want to support by funding nonprofits? How can government officials decide which nonprofits to fund? How can they determine the appropriate level of funding?

Unfortunately there is no one right answer or practice; a process that works well in one jurisdiction may be ill-suited to another. This guidebook does not suggest a single, one-size-fits-all solution for nonprofit funding. Instead, it suggests six questions local officials should ask when designing a process for funding nonprofits.

Elected officials and staff may ask, "Isn't there an easier way to do this?" Answering all the questions posed in this guidebook may take a lot of meetings and discussions and may generate disagreements as decision makers progress toward a single, useful product. However, if key stakeholders, especially elected officials, do not participate in the design of the process, it always will be subject to challenge, circumvention, or revision.

Comparing the relative merits of nonprofit applications for funds is challenging. Decision makers face difficult choices concerning different groups of people in need (such as youth, the working poor, and senior citizens) and competing political interests (for example, the arts, economic development, and human services). Criteria to consider include the government's goals and the organizational capacity of individual nonprofits to achieve those goals. Each local government must determine the specific priorities and issues to be addressed in deciding how to disburse public funds.

Having to allocate limited resources among many worthy efforts is understandably frustrating. Decision makers may be tempted to take out their frustration on nonprofits by not engaging in a fully impartial or deliberate evaluation process. The dilemma local government officials face is not that there are too many nonprofits, but, rather, how to allocate scarce public funds among so many worthy efforts. Nonprofits can articulate existing community needs and present innovative opportunities for addressing those needs in a manner that can assist local governments in navigating this difficult and sometimes contentious process.

As public officials consider funding nonprofits, the following six questions can direct their deliberations.

1. What benefits do government officials see in funding nonprofits?

Governments can tie funding of nonprofits to general or specific public goals, but doing either requires that elected officials and government staff clarify their reasons for funding nonprofits. With such clarification, discussions about allocations may focus on larger community goals rather than on the circumstances of individual nonprofits or specific people. Explicit consideration of why local officials want to fund nonprofits can help these officials determine whether their reasons are sufficient for continuing that support.

Clarifying reasons for funding nonprofits also changes how governments view nonprofits. Rather than regarding nonprofit funding as "charity" or "gifts," local governments may begin to perceive it as an alternative way to provide valuable community services by partnering with other organizations.

However, a local government might *not* want to fund nonprofits. Government officials might

- decide the government can provide the same services more effectively or less expensively.
- prefer to devote resources to government departments, even if services are not as effective or efficient.
- prefer not to devote staff time and attention to oversight of partnerships with nonprofits.
- fear making nonprofits dependent on government funding.
- want to cut spending instead of providing the service.

Officials should examine each reason to determine if the assumptions on which it is based are correct. For example, officials might assume that funding a community service through government departments is more efficient than funding nonprofits to provide the service. However, by using volunteers and supplemental grant money from outside sources, a nonprofit might deliver the same services less expensively than the government can.

In addition, avoiding funding community services through nonprofits simply because it "never has been done that way" ignores a growing national trend that encourages community problem-solving and broad collaboration among governments, nonprofits, the faith community, and the private sector. Most North Carolina local governments do, in fact, fund nonprofits to some degree. Understanding the purposes behind that funding will help public officials (and citizens) make better funding decisions.

2. Why should government officials have a formal process for making funding decisions?

The credibility of a local government's final funding choices depends in part on how the government makes the decision: who decides, what information the decision makers receive, what opportunities exist for community input, and how the entire process is perceived by the public. A decision-making process can serve a variety of purposes. It can

- demonstrate fairness.
- encourage citizen input.
- maximize accountability.
- minimize negative consequences or public criticism.
- streamline decision making.
- help a local government coordinate decision making with other local funders.
- help a government determine whether the nonprofit
  can achieve the government's goals.

Some of these purposes may conflict with each other. To design a process that will work well for the community, officials must identify, clarify, and address their reasons for creating the process. Then they should select procedures and practices that will help them achieve their intentions. Officials should carefully evaluate the implications of every decision they make during the process, because each will present advantages and disadvantages. For example, a process that employs a broad volunteer advisory group to review applications may elicit more citizen input but require additional staff resources to manage. A process that invites applications for any kind of proposal might provide opportunities for extensive participation but furnish less strategic direction for nonprofit funding.

3. How will government officials identify community needs they want to help nonprofits address?

If a government does not gather information about specific community needs, meeting those needs is likely to be accidental rather than deliberate. Local officials can learn about public issues people want the government to address in several ways. First, these officials might compile information that staff and elected officials have accumulated in the course of their contacts with citizens. For example, departments can be asked to list priorities for services in their areas of responsibility. Some local governments do this as part of their annual budget-preparation process. Elected officials sometimes use work sessions or retreats to develop lists of priorities for government action. Both government staff and elected officials can gain insight into community needs simply by doing their normal work. If, however, their perspectives do not encompass the diversity within a community or if they fail to become connected with and informed about underrepresented local groups, they may overlook relevant information or new trends.

Second, local governments can learn about community needs by seeking input from nonprofits or the broader community. Asking nonprofits to provide information about community needs places the burden of determining and describing those needs on the nonprofit and therefore lowers information-gathering costs for the local government. However, this alternative can be subject to bias if it favors politically savvy nonprofits. Legitimate community needs of invisible, disenfranchised, or unsophisticated populations may be particularly difficult to identify. Public hearings, community forums, and other opportunities for citizens to express their views can provide a broader assessment of community needs.

If one of the reasons for developing a formal funding process is to encourage citizen input, more transparent, inclusive methods of gathering information may be preferable. If streamlining decision making is a goal, relying on nonprofits to identify and document needs might be more appropriate. An informal process of exchanging information may be all that is necessary to gather comprehensive data on needs if a community is relatively small and provides regular opportunities for conversation among diverse stakeholders. This approach may not work as well in larger or more urban areas.

More formal methods of needs assessment include focus groups or surveys of carefully selected samples of the population. Although this approach is more costly, the expense might be shared among local funders such as the United Way, community foundations, and other governments. A joint needs assessment might be particularly useful if one of the reasons for developing a formal process is to coordinate funding with other local funders.

4. How will government officials obtain nonprofit proposals for meeting community needs?

Just as advertising may increase attendance at a special public event, how governments invite funding proposals may determine what they receive. Again, community characteristics, such as the size of the local population or diversity in political philosophies, might drive how a government decides to conduct this process. In a small community, government staff can simply call or send letters to the nonprofits telling them it is time to submit proposals. In more populous areas, it might be necessary to use a variety of media for the notification—for example, letters, public notices, newspapers, websites, or listservs.

If the government has numerous and diverse purposes for funding nonprofits, it may want to offer all local nonprofits the opportunity to submit proposals. If, however, the purposes are relatively narrow, contacting the nonprofits that are relevant to the identified goals may be sufficient.

A government can ask nonprofits to apply for funding in either of two ways. By issuing a request for applications (RFA), the local government can inform nonprofits about the opportunity and the process to apply for funding for programs the nonprofits decide will address public purposes. In a request for proposals (RFP), the government specifically defines the target of service (certain populations or certain desired outcomes, for example) in addition to sharing information about the funding process. In either case, the expectations for submitting applications should be explicit and easy to find and should specify the due date of the application, its format and content, the number of copies required, and so forth.

5. How will government officials review proposals?

Government staff, community volunteers, or elected officials might review proposals. The decision as to who should do so will reflect governing board concerns about such issues as timing, efficiency, program goals, previous experience with and level of trust in potential reviewers, delegation of various aspects of program design and execution, and balance between program goals and resource allocation parameters.

If staff manage the review, the government might ensure that the work of nonprofits will assist it in achieving specific predetermined community objectives. This option also might provide the quickest, most easily controlled, and most consistent evaluation process. However, if the same staff members perform the reviews year after year, this option may perpetuate previously established and familiar funding practices or preclude the infusion of new perspectives or ideas by entities outside the funding organization.

A volunteer board could screen applications for the council or the commissioners and might be able to alleviate political pressure on staff and elected officials. This strategy relies on citizens who are able and willing to donate many hours of their time for this purpose. To use a volunteer board effectively, a government should allocate funds for staff support and guidance, be willing to share decision-making authority with the volunteers, and allow adequate time for the volunteers to make their recommendations.

Having elected officials review and rate the applications increases community influence in the process and saves some direct staff costs. On the other hand, elected officials might be swayed by the interpersonal dynamics of their board or by the interests of a few vocal or well-connected constituents.

By using some combination of these structures, a community might agree on the relative priority of certain goals and deal realistically with the limits of its own resources. For example, a board that values developing a broad perspective on any important issue might ask both department heads and a volunteer advisory board to review applications and make suggestions for funding to the town or county manager. The manager might then make a final balanced recommendation to the elected board.

No matter who is involved in the review of proposals, the government must also balance its need for consistency over time with its interest in seeking innovation or new perspectives. Using the same decision makers and procedures every year might create a public perception of reliability in the process, but it could also foster an environment of stagnation or exclusivity as well.

6. How will government officials make funding decisions?

The elected governing board is ultimately responsible for making funding decisions, and it does so through adoption of a budget ordinance. But the governing board may set up procedures for subordinate groups to allocate the funds it authorizes. For example, some governing boards authorize a certain amount of funding for nonprofits and ask a citizen advisory committee or a staff task force to recommend how to allocate those funds.

Publicly supported criteria and procedures for deciding which nonprofits to fund, and at what levels, can help relieve boards of some of the political pressure they may face in making those decisions. Clarity about who will decide and on what basis decisions will be made is important to good relationships both inside and outside government. Changing procedures in the middle of budget review can produce mistrust and resentment. If the board wants to retain full flexibility to decide on nonprofit funding, it should clearly state that at the beginning of the process.

Tips for Creating Effective Funding Processes

- Define clearly at the outset how you will make funding decisions. Ensure that the criteria or standards for awarding funds are shared with applicants as well as with decision makers.
- Clearly state all expectations related to due date, format, content, and delivery of the applications.
- Assign staff to manage the logistics of the funding process.
- Use a broad-based, flexible strategic plan that includes goals nonprofits are expected to achieve.
- Avoid personal or professional biases.

- As early as possible, share information regarding the total funding available and the process for application with all nonprofits and the public.
- Use the same application process for all nonprofits seeking funding.
- Provide opportunities for input from citizens who represent the community.
- Coordinate with other local governments, foundations, and other community funders to use the same application form and, if possible, hold consolidated hearings to receive funding requests.[1]
- After the decisions are made, share information publicly about the amounts that nonprofits sought and received.
- Share information about the decision-making process equally and openly within the community.

Steps to Fund Nonprofits

Each of the steps below is followed by strategies elected officials often cite. These responses may be useful guides for deliberation, but board members should explore fully their own ideas with regard to each step.

- Define the government's reasons for appropriating funds for nonprofits.
  - To help meet public needs not addressed by local government programs
  - To augment existing local government services
  - To help meet specific local government goals
- Define the government's objectives for the decision-making process.
  - To create a fair process
  - To include citizen input
  - To maximize accountability
  - To minimize negative consequences
  - To streamline decision making
  - To coordinate decision making with other local funders
  - To fund nonprofits that will achieve the government's objectives

1. Although the government mandates of cities and counties may differ, overlapping goals might make working across organizational boundaries worthwhile. Philanthropies may have similar strategic interests as well. In general, a community is likely to benefit from both procedural efficiencies and strategic focus if all public funders share information and coordinate processes related to the nonprofits.

- Define how the government will assess needs or gather information.
  - Rely on nonprofits to present needs to government in formal proposals
  - Rely on the knowledge of government staff and elected officials
  - Rely on citizens to identify needs and inform the government of them
  - Search for information informally through community contacts
  - Conduct a needs assessment to collect data directly or partner with others doing community needs assessments
- Decide how to obtain proposals from nonprofits.
  - Let the nonprofits take the initiative
  - Have government staff or elected officials notify particular nonprofits
  - Put out a formal notification, a request for applications, or a request for proposals to all nonprofits or the whole community
- Evaluate how various processes for making funding decisions support identified goals. Any of the following groups, or various combinations of them, can participate in the review of proposals and recommendations for funding.
  - Local government staff
  - Community volunteers
  - Standing advisory boards
  - Members of the elected body
- Determine the preference of elected officials.
  - Do they want to make the funding decisions themselves?
  - Would they rather defer the funding decisions to staff or volunteers?

WORKSHEET: *Our Nonprofit Funding Process*

What is our purpose in appropriating funds to nonprofits?

_____

_____

_____

What are our goals for the decision-making process?

_____

_____

_____

How will we assess needs or gather information?

_____

_____

_____

How will we obtain proposals from nonprofits?

_____

_____

_____

How will the ways we make funding decisions support our identified goals?

_____

_____

_____

How will administrative staff be involved in deciding how to fund nonprofits?

_____

_____

_____

Checklist for Drafting Nonprofit Funding Requests for Applications (RFAs) or Requests for Proposals (RFPs)

1. Getting Started
- ❑ Find a template ("go-by").
  - ❑ Check your own files.
  - ❑ Use Google or other search engines (search for "requests for applications" or "requests for proposals").
  - ❑ Ask knowledgeable, experienced colleagues.
- ❑ Gather information that clarifies the funding goals (including any specific products, services, or results you expect the nonprofit to provide).

2. Document Substance
- ❑ If you are using a document from another source as your template, carefully search for and remove all references and information that are not parts of your current request (for example, other government or entity names, contact information, or Terms & Conditions used by the other government or entity).
- ❑ Define key terms in a Definitions section.
  - ❑ Spell and reference defined terms correctly throughout your document.
  - ❑ Capitalize, bold, or italicize all defined terms throughout your document.
- ❑ In drafting your request, use what you've learned about community needs; goals of elected officials or government departments; and any specific products, services, or results you expect the nonprofit to provide. Minimum requirements should be broad enough to include as many providers as possible but specific enough to fit your community's needs.
- ❑ Be clear, simple, and accurate.
  - ❑ Avoid legalese and fancy-sounding words when possible.
  - ❑ Use "shall" and "must"—not "should" or "may"—when imposing a requirement or duty.
- ❑ Use the active voice instead of the passive voice when possible, because it clarifies who must do what (Replace "The following documents must be submitted . . ." with "Applicant must submit the following documents . . .").
- ❑ Ensure your evaluation criteria are clear and easy to find.

❏ Use standard terms and conditions that were recently reviewed and approved by your attorney (preferably within the last year).

❏ Make sure all key information (such as contact person name, dates for application submission, and mailing addresses for submission) is accurate and consistent throughout the document.

3. Document Format

❏ Use a short and descriptive document title (for example, "Carolina County Request for Applications for 2010–11 Fiscal Year").

❏ Create a header or footer (with the document title, entity name, and due date and time) that appears on each page.

❏ Place page numbers ("page X of Y") on each page.

❏ State clearly and conspicuously the number of copies required (for example, "Please provide the original plus 5 copies.").

❏ Specify whether electronic submission is acceptable, and, if so, what format is required.

❏ Double-check contact information (phone numbers, e-mail addresses, and street or P.O. Box addresses) for typos.

❏ Use short but descriptive section headings (for example, use "Evaluation Criteria" rather than "Funding Decision" as a heading for the section outlining your evaluation criteria).

❏ Format your headings, sections, and subsections in a consistent and easy-to-follow manner.

❏ Replace all slashes ("/") with an "and" or "or."

❏ Check the entire document for typos and spelling errors.

❏ Check the document for reading ease (aim for 60 to 70 points on the Flesch Reading Ease scale, or for a score of 7 to 8 on the Flesch-Kincaid Grade Level score).[2]

2. Microsoft Word will check your documents for reading ease. For Word 2003 users: on the Tools menu, click Options, then Spelling & Grammar; select the Check grammar with spelling check box; select the Show readability statistics check box, and then click OK; on the Standard toolbar, click the Spelling & Grammar button to see the readability statistics after the spelling and grammar review is completed. For Word 2007 users: on the Review tab, click Spelling & Grammar; click Options in the bottom left-hand corner of the window; in the next window, select the Show readability statistics check box (under When correcting spelling and grammar in Word you may have to first check Check grammar with spelling); click Recheck document, and then click OK.

❏ Get a "fresh eyes" review: someone who did not participate in drafting the document should read it for inconsistencies, typos, errors, and comprehension.

❏ Finally, review cross-references to headings and sections for accuracy.

Notes about Drafts:

- Save drafts with a document name that includes the date and the initials of the person who most recently edited the draft (for example, RFA_31Dec2010_EY). This will help to ensure that changes are made only to the most current version of each draft.

- Be aware that your drafts are public records.

Accountability

Accountability expectations establish performance responsibilities, responsiveness limits, reporting relationships, and review authority for both local governments and nonprofits. Sometimes a government creates these expectations and presents them to a nonprofit as conditions for working together. Sometimes negotiations produce accountability expectations. Mutual accountability is particularly appropriate when governments and nonprofits need to learn from each other and from experience how to better serve the public.

Effective accountability in partnerships is multidirectional and multidimensional. Governments and nonprofits can design new accountability patterns if they are willing to share decision-making, take time to deliberate and experiment, and respect the different perspectives of the organizational representatives. Using the model of mutual accountability, the challenge for community partners is to move beyond the limited buyer–seller relationship often embodied in government–nonprofit contracts and to move toward real collaboration—ongoing, shared responsibility for improving public services.

The general public commonly equates "accountability" with "fiscal integrity" and focuses on finances instead of fairness and on process rather than performance. While financial accountability in relationships with nonprofits is important, limiting accountability to finances is inadequate when trying to ensure that the services the community wants and needs are provided effectively. A more service-oriented focus regards accountability goals as multidimensional, addressing three general categories.

- **Fairness.** Standards apply to all people equally, whether a standard involves hiring practices for staff or eligibility criteria for clients. Fair decisions are made according to impartial standards and not based on favoritism.
- **Performance**. Activities are carried out successfully and produce the intended results.
- **Financial integrity.** Funds are administered in an honest and responsible manner, commonly in accordance with generally accepted accounting principles.

All three categories are important and should be considered in any comprehensive approach to defining and implementing accountability. To ensure that all three goals for accountability are addressed, a local government must make them explicit. That is, key stakeholders must discuss their expectations about fairness, finances, and performance and build these expectations into the tools used to manage the relationship. Discussions about mutual expectations and the contracts, reports, audits, and one-to-one contacts that reflect those expectations should address all three goals.

Often, setting accountability expectations and monitoring how well they are met are both accomplished independently by government and nonprofit staffs. Each assesses accountability on its own and decides whether and how it wants to continue the working relationship with the other entity. This unilateral approach limits the ability of governments and nonprofits to learn from each other but may save staff time and effort. If the transaction is a one-time purchase and the government has no reason to develop trust in the vendor, then hierarchical accountability may be appropriate. Collaboration is neither sought nor needed. Often, however, governments and their nonprofit partners are exploring ways to address broad public problems together. If both entities want to refine their expectations of each other and develop more effective ways to serve the public, they may choose to work together in revising their accountability expectations. Trusting each other helps sustain effective partnerships.

Mutual accountability can improve public service as key stakeholders review a government–nonprofit relationship and decide how to change it. By reviewing their accountability expectations together, the parties can refine and revise those expectations to fit new circumstances or challenges. This process can be time-consuming and difficult but will be worth the extra effort if government and nonprofit partners learn how to effectively address important public needs that neither party could meet alone. Mutual accountability can shift the focus from surveillance to service.

Tips for Developing Mutual Accountability

- Determine whether both the local government and the nonprofit are willing to take responsibility for ensuring fairness, performance, and financial integrity.
- Work through the questions in the Expectations for Mutual Accountability worksheet, opposite. Putting the answers into practice constitutes accountability.
- Recognize that, often, managing accountability is an appropriate role for staff members. Elected local government officials should focus on clarifying their reasons for funding nonprofits and understanding the gains they expect to achieve. The details of managing the accountability process can be delegated to staff.

WORKSHEET: *Expectations for Mutual Accountability*

This exercise offers one way to define mutual expectations about future interactions in a local government–nonprofit partnership. Discuss the following four questions as they relate to the mutual-accountability dimensions of fairness, performance, and financial integrity.

Product. Who is expected to carry out which actions, and for whom?
In relation to fairness:

_____

_____

_____

In relation to performance:

_____

_____

_____

In relation to financial responsibility:

_____

_____

_____

Alteration. Who can invoke or alter these expectations?
In relation to fairness:

_____

_____

_____

In relation to performance:

_____

_____

_____

In relation to financial responsibility:

_____

_____

_____

Information. Who should provide what information to whom about how responsibilities are fulfilled?

In relation to fairness:

_____

_____

_____

In relation to performance:

_____

_____

_____

In relation to financial responsibility:

_____

_____

_____

Review. Who is expected to use what information to make decisions about the future of the relationship?

In relation to fairness:

_____

_____

_____

In relation to performance:

_____

_____

_____

In relation to financial responsibility:

_____

_____

_____

Strengthening Relationships between Local Governments and Nonprofits

Local government and nonprofit organizations frequently serve the same clients, address the same community problems, and can often support each other. Although the perspectives of the two sectors frequently differ, they are potentially complementary. The challenge for both entities is to find ways to work together that permit them to fulfill their unique responsibilities while complementing each other's work. However, the differences between the two sectors—in organizational structure and culture, for example—can create tension or obstacles. Local governments are subject to laws and regulations concerning financial management and other areas that do not apply to nonprofit or other private corporations. Also, local government officials must solicit and consider the viewpoints of many citizens and balance competing views from throughout their communities. Conversely, many nonprofit organizations rely largely on volunteers committed to the specific cause their organization addresses. Nonprofits can be attractive to local governments as a way to try out new or pilot programs because they can react and implement services quickly. Yet this same characteristic—the ability to move quickly—can be perceived by local governments as a liability because all the necessary viewpoints may not be considered.

Close collaboration can help strike the balance between nonprofits' focus on a particular set of issues and the need for local governments to consider a broad range of interests and concerns affecting the entire community. Collaboration between nonprofit organizations and local governments is most effective when

- the focus is on one issue,
- the goals are clearly defined,
- representatives of all the stakeholders are involved in the problem-solving process, and
- time and resources are available to support planning.

Because developing and maintaining true collaboration is so difficult, both nonprofits and local governments should explore just how closely they want and can afford to work together. Both can benefit from a joint evaluation of their current connections and a joint decision about how connected they would like to be in relation to what activities and concerning which issues. Furthermore, both must identify, evaluate, and set limits on the resources they are willing to expend to work more closely together.

There is no one right relationship between governments and nonprofit organizations. Indeed, within a community the relationship may shift as different issues or events arise. Also, relationships will vary among communities. Each partnership must decide for itself how to achieve the most effective balance of independence and connection. The optimal degree and type of connection depend on each community's situation.

Local governments and nonprofits trying to build effective partnerships face several obstacles: different perceptions about the same situations; a lack of understanding of each other's work; the effects of the economic and cultural base of a community on the style of communication, information sharing, and decision making; and an imbalance of power in relationships. Frequent and accurate communication can help to overcome these obstacles.

Navigating the tensions between nonprofit organizations and local governments can be a challenge for any community. Like any segment of the population, people in the public sector represent a broad diversity of expertise, professional skills, styles of interpersonal communication, and level of passion for their work. This diversity may be viewed either with suspicion and rigidity or with celebration and possibly amusement. By using their differences constructively, people who work in local governments and nonprofit organizations can draw on each other's strengths to help compensate for their weaknesses. Together they may be able to serve the public more effectively than either sector could alone.

Tips for Strengthening Relationships
What Local Governments Can Do

❏ Minimize the mistrust, frustration, or misunderstanding nonprofits experience during budget planning by sharing information about funding, including information about the following:

- The amount of money available
- Government priorities
- The application and evaluation process
- Criteria to be used in reviewing applications
- The expectations for reporting and accountability

❏ Coordinate nonprofit organizations' funding applications and presentations to the local government with those to the United Way or other local private-sector grant makers to minimize duplication of effort and to improve communication among local funders.

❑ View problems or needs as belonging to the whole community, not just to a nonprofit.

- Recognize that the clients of nonprofit organizations are community members deserving of resources.
- Express appreciation for the missions of nonprofit organizations.

❑ Acknowledge nonprofit organizations as serious businesses.

- Recognize the value that professional, paid employees can bring to an organization.
- Support nonprofits in their efforts to strengthen internal professionalism.
- Consider the impact that the payrolls and programs of nonprofit organizations can have on the local economy.

What Nonprofits and Local Governments Can Do Together

❑ Share information, both during and outside day-to-day working relationships.

- Sponsor an annual human services forum that includes government and nonprofit staff, elected officials, and community volunteers.
- Undertake joint strategic planning efforts, especially around specific issues such as homelessness or juvenile delinquency.
- Collaborate on community needs assessments.
- Consider locating varied services that serve the same population at the same site.
- Hold regular meetings among nonprofit organization directors, county department heads, and program staff of both organizations.

❑ Share resources.

- Invite staff of the other type of organization to participate in training opportunities your organization typically offers.
- Offer to share expertise by providing training to or by meeting with staff of the other type of organization.
- Invite program staff from other organizations to meet in your facility.
- Make it possible for your staff to serve on community boards, committees, and task forces.
- Make second-hand furniture or equipment available for others to use.

❏ Jointly develop clear, written guidelines about mutual expectations and work to be accomplished together.

❏ Recognize that each organization can be the other's best support for understanding and handling the stress associated with working in the public sector. Local governments and nonprofits are dealing with similar challenges.

Conclusion

Local governments may work with nonprofit organizations for a variety of reasons and in a variety of ways. One of the most common kinds of relationships involves funding, whether via grants, appropriations, purchase-of-service contracts, or other kinds of assistance. Governments must observe legal restrictions when making funding choices, but, in general, governments may fund a nonprofit to provide any services that fulfill a "public purpose." A local government might decide to partner with a nonprofit to take advantage of the nonprofit's expertise, flexibility, capacity, efficiency, or community connections. In designing a funding process, governments should consider their reasons for funding nonprofits, their reasons for having a formal funding process, a plan for identifying community needs that nonprofits can help address, a plan for obtaining funding proposals, and a plan for reviewing and making decisions on those proposals. Careful deliberation about these issues takes effort but can help create effective funding procedures.

When governments and nonprofits expect to have an ongoing relationship, they should use a mutual accountability model and work together to craft expectations about how the project or program will be funded, monitored, and evaluated. This kind of collaboration can also foster good communication, an important part of strong relationships between governments and nonprofits. The different perspectives, positions, and cultures of these two sectors can lead to tension and strained relationships. Yet governments and nonprofits are both working to improve the community and often face similar challenges in doing so. Learning to work together effectively can help both organizations better serve their communities.

Notes

Much of the information in this guidebook was taken from the following articles, which are also available online at www.publicintersection.unc.edu on the Publications page. All of the articles were originally published in *Popular Government*, a publication of the School of Government.

Altman-Sauer, Lydian, Margaret Henderson, and Gordon Whitaker. "Building Community Capacity to Meet Public Needs." *Popular Government* 70, no. 2 (Winter 2005).

Altman-Sauer, Lydian, Margaret Henderson, and Gordon P. Whitaker. "Strengthening Relationships between Local Governments and Nonprofits." *Popular Government* 66, no. 2 (Winter 2001).

Bluestein, Frayda, and Anita R. Brown-Graham. "Local Government Contracts with Nonprofit Organizations: Questions and Answers." *Popular Government* 67, no. 1 (Fall 2001).

Henderson, Margaret, Lydian Altman-Sauer, and Gordon Whitaker. "Deciding to Fund Nonprofits: Key Questions." *Popular Government* 67, no. 4 (Summer 2002).

Henderson, Margaret, Gordon P. Whitaker, and Lydian Altman-Sauer. "Establishing Mutual Accountability in Nonprofit–Government Relationships." *Popular Government* 69, no. 1 (Fall 2003).

Whitaker, Gordon, and Rosalind Day. "How Local Governments Work with Nonprofits in North Carolina." *Popular Government* 66, no. 2 (Winter 2001).

Additional resources available through the School of Government include:

Gulati-Partee, Gita. "A Primer on Nonprofit Organizations." *Popular Government* 66, no. 4 (Summer 2001).

Whitaker, Gordon P., and James C. Drennan. "Local Government and Nonprofit Organizations." Article 11 in *County and Municipal Government in North Carolina*. www.sog.unc.edu/pubs/cmg/.